Loving Characters Into
...tation Snacks

...ványi &
...a van Gorkum

ROUGH TRADE BOOKS

@shelleyduvall88

Elsene, Brussels
Hoofdstedelijk Gewest

LOVING CHARACTERS

Sober scorpio hidden under Brussels' autumn leaves in search of librarian, linguist, lover of literature to teach me the terminology of online dating. I offer: a visit to Marcel Broothaers buried in my backyard, contemplations on your interior, an unpacked box filled with bondage rope, a velvet cave

@brunettestreep

Amsterdam,
Netherlands

INTO GAS STATION SNACKS

Expect the darkest sense of humor. Alone most of the time, but would like to spend some of it with like minds that can low-key swerve any topic into the gutter. Independent, read a lot, walk everywhere. Open to all genders for chats or more.

MESSAGES

Fri 12:23am

hi shelleyduvall88,

sober, bi, brunette meryl streep scorpio hiding in plain sight in amsterdam. i speak five languages, write, and have a very big book case, but still google most of the terminology here, and this is my first dating app. art and graves are my segue into unpacking the self and contemplating being tied up :) what else do you do down there?

Dear Meryl,

You got me distracted from my homework. I am supposed to prepare a class for a group of girls on verbs for positions and prepositions - in Dutch, that is. Teaching language to the unemployed is my current occupation. However, I think the core of my job is mostly to navigate the social complexity and fragility of groups of people who ended up being in a class together and to keep conversations going. And then I would say I'm playing the role of the teacher, as, in my other life, I prefer to hide - as you put it so well - in plain sight. What is your camouflage?

With love, Shelley

Dear Meryl,

You got me distracted from my homework. I am supposed to prepare a class for a group of girls on verbs for positions and prepositions - in Dutch, that is. Teaching language to the unemployed is my current occupation. However, I think the core of my job is mostly to navigate the social complexity and fragility of groups of people who ended up being in a class together and to keep conversations going. And then I would say I'm playing the role of the teacher, as, in my other life, I prefer to hide - as you put it so well - in plain sight. What is your camouflage?

With love, Shelley

Dear Meryl,

You got me distracted from my homework. I am supposed to prepare a class on verbs for positions and prepositions for a bunch of girls - in Dutch that is. Teaching language to the unemployed is my current occupation, although I would say that the core of my job is to navigate the social complexity and fragility of a group of people who ended up being in a class together and to keep conversation going. And then I would say that I'm mostly playing the role of the teacher, as in my other life, I prefer to - as you put it so well - hide in plain sight. What is your camouflage?

With love, Shelley

Dear Meryl, my apologies for sending the same message multiple times. This app is not working so well for me.

I didn't mind reading it three times. Did you finish your homework? Prepositions are my undoing. As far as camouflage goes, hiding takes two. I'm an artist and writer with a job, somewhat late to the party on both fronts, but independent thanks to the latter with more free time than not to pursue the first. Tell me more about yourself, your current view or fantasy if you feel like it. No rush.

Sat 08:27pm

Your questions about my current view/fantasy caused a (small) existential crisis, which is why it took me relatively long to answer. How to explain these things to a stranger on a dating app? It is perhaps helpful to tell you that I am sometimes an artist - I was early to the party - when I am not a language teacher. However,

I don't do multitasking, so it's either the one or the other. Until june of this year I was a visual artist participating in a post-master program in Brussels in the field of artistic research. Until the end of march I'm a language teacher, and from april I am someone with a temporary guest studio in an artists initiative in Rotterdam. I am not sure if I want to be there as an artist, and do the opposite of you: I try to figure out how to transition into writing. The question 'what is your current view' is tricky, since I am, in my practice, mostly concerned with disorientation, a lack of view/vision/overview, and trying to understand how to live with instability and not knowing what to think. This thought process happens in a SketchUp file, and part of my practice consists if being a tour guide in virtual space. I am now going to press send, and continue after the break with some details about my day, and try to come up with something to get information from you, attempting to avoid exchanging trivia (although I have a soft spot for detailed descriptions of the logistics of other people's lives)

Details: I ran in the forest, in sunlight and fog, ran past a kiosk, a table set up with oysters waiting to be eaten by my fellow bourgeois visitors of the park, many dogs, babies, birds, after spending time with some friends and their babies in a bar - I was impatient and left soon, feeling no need for social interaction after a week spent talking - went to a bookshop, bought Sheila Heti's Motherhood and 'Things I don't want to know' by Deborah Levy, searched for a bus stop for a while, hungry, surrounded by tons of people on the christmas market, people singing on a stage, irritated, bus stop was not served, shared a table with some kids at an overcrowded Burger King to prevent fainting on my journey home, ate a burger that was supposedly vegetarian, continued my search for a bus, an old lady at the busstop to her husband: "there are many busses stopping at central station," I thought about the trashcan at the burger king saying "serving trays make me nauseous," and worried about the phenomenon of objects speaking to us, got home, bought eggs, currently listen to Nick Cave.

What does an invisible person do with this capscity on a saturday night? And tell me something trivial :)

:) a small, existential crisis was not my intention. I'm enjoying your detailed description of your day, the way your thoughts dip above and below the surface of your surroundings. I will think about your questions and get back to you with a response worthy of talking trash cans and trays at Burger King.

In the meantime; I'm watching Five Easy Pieces with Jack Nicholson and randomly talking to two other people here on lex who are (or seem) complete opposites of you and each other. One is a vague guy who speaks in cosmic metaphors, the other a sadistic woman in Oklahoma who is spontaneously sharing some shocking things with me that warm my heart because it is happening on this app, and perhaps also because she is in Oklahoma. Next to me are crackers, tangerines and a hot chocolate I made with hot water and honey, a space foam pillow and a copy of Elephant magazine I am going to cut up for work.

Sun 10:55pm

Your art/practice intrigues me. the matter of disorientation, virtual worlds and being a tour guide in that sounds very dynamic in that it is highly specific and yet you can take it in so many directions. Back in art school I was introduced to the work of Saskia Olde Wolbers. Are you familiar with her work? She creates worlds out of found objects, submerges them in a water basin in her studio and films them. there is always a voice over that tells a story while the film shows these strange, abstract, uninhabited worlds that look life size, but don't always look real. that is one of the strengths of her work; the tension of something real looking unreal, small looking big, etc. the worlds she creates move between convincing and abstract. these tensions are a form of disorientation, i think. which artists do you like?

details : I walked in the cold sun, the light was flat. worked in my studio, and in the evening cleaned my house while listening to Blue Velvet by Lynch on my headphones. there are many more things in your messages i want to respond to, but right now I'm tired. i'll write better 'trivial' details next time. and tell me more about yours.

Carried your tangerines with me today, made pumpkin soup. Was very proud and happy with the result until I tasted it: bitter vomit. Up til 5 minutes ago I thought Elephant magazine was a magazine about...elephants. The image of you, cutting up elephants on a saturday night while eating crackers was pleasing, and I imagined you as a collage artist, making landscapes out of national geographic magazine. And then I imagined meeting you one day, and you would ask for my professional opinion on your collages of wild animals, and I probably wouldn't know what to say. Is there any glitter included? I hope so. And it sounds like you found your virtual guru through this app. What's his prediction for 2020? Not sure how to imagine sadism and sharing shocking intimacies though. Does she punish you when you show empathy? Cut your lines? Send you gifs of burning puppies?

Oh no, I read back my message and saw that I missed one of yours! I will retroactively reply to those later.

Mon 09:44am

I don't divulge other people's intimate confessions, even if they are anonymous strangers on the other side of the world. you are going to have to find out for yourself what it might entail to chat with a sadistic woman you don't know, but share a language with.

sorry about your culinary-improv misadventure. turning pumpkin into soup sounds laboursome and i applaud the effort, but encourage (healthy?) takeout. It was amusing and mildly horrifying to imagine myself making animal collages and/or using glitter. neither could be further from the truth, but if the glitter is something you are personally interested in, i'm listening. at the moment i'm standing in my clean kitchen. the light is beautiful, as always. Dutch light has this way of being warm in the sky and cold on what it falls on, and vice versa. this is one of those mornings; the sky is blue and white and my kitchen is bathed in a pink hue. im eating an apple from the fridge and drinking my favourite italian coffee w a bit of milk i don't bother to heat.

I'm sorry if I came across as rude or nosy. My apologies, other peoples intimacies are none of my business indeed. I am currently taking a break from glitter, for it is a celebration on camera I share with a friend, and we seem to be living in bubbles that cannot get close at the moment. I carried some red glitters in my ears for years, after a glitter feast with her in a Swedish forest. Some have entered my brain I'm sure. I enjoyed the start of your day, your description made me want to be that apple and that italian coffee.

Thank you for introducing me to Saskia Olde Wolbers, it is new to me. I have only looked at it briefly on the small screen of my phone. Will take a closer look later. I find it difficult to tell what artists I really like, because many of them I liked only temporary. I can tell you works/artists that I consider the cornerstones of my practice. I think I am attached to them because of encountering them when in art school, I was very young, everything was new and I could be hit very hard: Gillian Wearing's 'Dancing in Peckham Palace', 'Break Down' by Michael Landy, all works by rene daniels - he had a show at Wiels recently, where I worked as an actual tour guide. I made an exhibition space with his work in my virtual studio, and, as part of a presentation in the context of the post master program, I performed the exact same tour through his exhibition, but now standing in front of a projection screen while navigating through a limitless space - 'Last Lecture' by Barbara Visser (you can find it on Ubu web), and then some. What does it mean for you to like an artist/writer/.., what place does it have? This can be quite literal I guess. Is it an active practice of engaging with a work? Do you have a database? Do you collect? Do you discard?

And I took your advice (partially) and got myself a frozen pizza from the organic shop. Nothing went wrong.

Last remark for today: your description of the Dutch light made me feel inarticulate in describing the Belgian light. Need to work on that.

Wed 08:40pm

I had a very long day yesterday of work after a sleepless night. I saw the sun rise and on the train I thought about you, imagined you in my kitchen and decided I have to think of something to whisper to the glitter that lives in your ear. Now I'm dressed and off to work again. Art talk will follow later.

My glitter awaits your whisper. Observation of the Belgian light on the 3rd and 4th of december, around 8:30 am: a muddled orange brown and a hue of purple tangles two corkscrew hazels outside outside my window with a courtyard formed by undistinguishable houses and -unlike the Dutch light - obscures more than it makes visible.

Thu 09:59pm

I will be hovering above the netherlands between 23rd of december and 5th of january. I am enjoying this conversation very much and I'm curious how this would work in real life. If you are more into chatting and not so much into meeting, don't worry about it. Otherwise, we could discuss art, glitter and animal collage over coffee, tea, lemonade or fresh air.

you are not inarticulate. i know that light. it belongs to a particular time of day more than it does to a place. it obscures so it can warp your sense of time and steal it. and on an earlier note, you are not rude. i wasn't offended at all. you can ask me whatever you want, but some things are not mine to tell.

i'm taking my time with your art references. thank you for those. i started with Break Down, which you introduced me to. It speaks to me, like many such works by other artists, but this one esp. stands out in its thoughtful execution, and because of him - the way he talks about it, how personal the work is. how even in this radical act of erasure he sometimes took objects off the disassembly line for some personal reason and stalled its destruction before putting it back further down the line. this work will stay with me, I'm sure.

I wish I'd have visited wiels then and had you as my tour guide. on the note of limitless spaces; today one of my favourite things happened. i woke up to a morning wedged by fog. it is one of the most magical phenomena to me because of its ability to obliterate all sense of boundaries. no wind, quiet, it turns the world into a different dimension of itself. is there such a thing as fog-fetish? nebulophilia?

tell me about your Brussels-days/nights. the little things you like to hear and write about.

I was writing this when your last message arrived. i want to meet you too, and also keep writing ;) I will be here and free from obligations after the 27th.

Saturday I'm going out to dance all night for the first time in a long time. i will report on the dark, sweaty, basement excursion.

Fri 09:04am

Let's meet on the 28th. I am going to give you my phone number, although I prefer to keep writing on this app, but just in case (it crashes/my phone gets stolen/my memory is suddenly erased/I forgot all languages/it's the end of the internet). Some context to my tendency to anticipate on an unknown future: I have grown up with a mother who thinks it's impossible to go out for dinner if you haven't made reservations (for, let's say, a mediocre italian restaurant) half a year in advance, and a father who prefers to fold out the - very large - fold-out table the day before christmas, because, what if it doesn't fold out when the guests (my aunt and uncle) are there? So here it is +32XXXXXXXX, and let's forget I did this three weeks in advance (but not until you have written this down on a slip of paper with a waterproof pen and put it in a safe place) and continue writing.

+31XXXXXXXXX and the 28th is good.

If I had known you were into fog I wouldn't have withheld you my tuesday morning I went for a run in a nearby forest to find a very thick fog resting on the field. As I continued my path uphill, a couple of meters into the distance all I could see, two boys on racing bikes passed by. In a quick glance I identified them as bratty art school boys who were on their way to some class on photography, this department being located in a small, light-pink villa at the back of the forest. Them both very muscular, the thighs of second boy reminded me of a lover when I was 22 and still in artschool myself, filled me with nostalgia. I ran further into familiar terrain hidden from sight, the ground nearly frozen, my hands turning red and my breath and some birds to be the only sound as I found them, the two boys, as I arrived on top of another hill, far below me in a valley their bikes embraced, bathing in the morning fog they kissed, endlessly, and they were all there was and what there needed to be, I crossed the valley, the open field their bedroom, turning myself into drops to not disturb, my sweat evaporating, invigorated I ran up another hill, filled with joy for them, this moment, their intimacy that we shared, in a haze.

can we meet in ams the 28th and are you a morning person? if so, i have an idea where we can meet.

Yes, we can meet in amsterdam and yes, since two years I am a morning person, so please hit me with your earliest hour.

won't be too early this time, but let's meet a bit before ten at quartier putain oudekerksplein 4.

Fog, knowing when and what to withhold, and this kind of writing are all buttons you just found.

Sat 02:23pm

when i was 'leetle' and growing up in Budapest, i spent all my weekends at my grandparents' house. there was a big hot water boiler on the wall above the bathtub and i used to love sitting in the tub for hours with a wooden drawing board laid across the top of the tub, reading all the magazines my grandfather bought faithfully every week, while eating snacks my grandmother made for me. it was a cylinder shaped boiler that had wide opening along the front where you could look into a small forest of blue flames. my favourite thing was to sit in the bath with the light switched off and just have the blue flames roaring as i kept the water running and pulled out the plug enough to fill it back up again. a bathtub is sadly not a part of my life now, but i love to shower in the dark, to recreate this feeling of boundless space, wilderness and fog, where i can't tell where my body ends and something else begins.

i also have a penchant to organize the details of my life, but for completely opposite reasons to the lovely family dynamic you describe. i come from a very colourful and utterly chaotic family. funny how these opposites trigger similar behaviour in both our cases.

I too like to shower in the dark. I too like baths, and imagining I am a reptile crawling through the sand that is the floor, discovering the bathtub as part of my habitat, spending some time there - entirely still, perhaps some limbs stretched out over the edges - before I slip out of it again and let my body dry in the sun that is the hairdryer and the towel. For one more week I'll stay in a home with a bath. Before you invited me to this bathroom of your childhood, I had been meaning to tell you about my friend who came to visit for the weekend, and that she had really wanted to take a hot bath and drink coffee while in it. So this morning I filled it for her, and brought her the coffee and went back to bed to read, and then remembered someone, an acquaintance I guess, telling me how she had mostly enjoyed her birthday party hearing her friends enjoying themselves while she herself was upstairs, taking a bath, and that facilitating and witnessing the party was to her the most pleasurable of the experience, and I said I understood - and it made me happy that my friends body was surrounded by water and mine by sheets, and we were co-existing in silence, alone with our thoughts. My hair is still wet from the bath I just took, and there is much more to say about the experience of being in a bathtub and while I was under water I thought of you and tried to experience the space the other way around - a tension of the water surface around my nose and lips - as if it was the water where I belonged and the cold air I was dipping my body into, and I wanted to feel safe and held by the air.

Another friend I spent the day with was born in Budapest and grew up in the netherlands. Yesterday evening she was describing her summers, when her family would return to hungary for the summer, how happy she was, to be a kid, and that she had this recurring dream in which she tries to travel back from budapest, but there is always something and she can never return.

When you mention your family I picture hers, that might be equally chaotic and colourful.

I'm having a hard time writing these messages, there's so many trails to follow and much to say.

I'm trying to imagine what garments will catch your sweat tonight, what shoes you will happily take off this morning, what underwear you'll fall asleep in.

do you want me to show you?

Soundtrack of my evening is Nick Cave's Ghosteen. Not so suitable for dancing, but it is for bathing, lying down on a couch in snakeskin, lace and cashmere

Yes

the red hand files/20.00 days on earth are wonderful. i will now blowdry my hair and brave the freezing night, and wait for a pic from you sometime.

20.000...

I spotted black feathers, which always makes me happy

do you still want to meet?

Sun 12:11am

Yes, of course I want to meet you! Sorry to leave you hanging there, my battery died.

Picture of me will follow tomorrow. I just decided to cut bangs again, and let's say, it still needs some work. My whatsapp picture is me, or, a painting of me - unfortunately I don't have a rainbow around me permanently.

I sent you pictures anyway. I look forward to your report of the caves, darkrooms, basements, loopholes you'll find yourself in tonight.

I'm glad you sent pictures. neither snakeskin nor an ushanka have ever looked so good on anyone.

The basement was fun, but I didn't stay long. All the shirtless, berghain type bratty boys reminded me of your forest run and my thoughts started drifting.

I am very much enjoying our conversation too, and agree that there are many things left to talk about.

My fantasy has given you raven's wings. It has been night since the day started, it is raining and I have given in to the darkness: I am in my bed, surrounded by various sources of entertainment and work. I imagine you lying in bed, one wing folded underneath your body the other spread out, turning the bed into a tent under which you read with a flashlight. I ran through the forest, now thinking about your bratty berghain boys, and wondered where your mind had drifted. The landscape changed dramatically in the last five days. Tuesday, the fog had covered for the loss of leaves, and now I could see through the trees and understood that all the times I had been running there, I had been unaware of the orientation of things - a football stadium appeared to be where I entered, though I had always experienced it to be far far away. Has it been day there? I like your curls.

Your fantasy is accurate; I adore corvids. I nurture a mild delusion that they see me as one of their own whenever I walk past them in the street.

I love the image you painted of me in bed reading under my own wing.

It was day here today, but not a long one. In the afternoon my eye caught the spine of the book 'Wittgenstein's Mistress', and in my fantasy I had found you a new name - at least in my phone this is your name, for now. Do you know the book? It is notoriously idiosyncratic; written as a long stream of consciousness, they are the thoughts of a woman who believes she is the last person on earth, retelling the story of her life.

don't you think this feeling of being a last person on earth is, on some level, inherent to all women? it might go unnamed, unnoticed, or in most cases replaced with the feeling of motherhood, but that is pure speculation on my part. perhaps you'll be able to shed light on this after reading Sheila Heti. in any case, there seemed to be a connection between Wittgenstein's Mistress and your way of writing about your days and surroundings.

At the club my thoughts, as usual, drifted indirectly towards sex. it was barely lit and foggy, there were lots of handsome boys half naked and fit, making out on the dancefloor under a pure blue strobe light. I imagined being in the forest with you as silent witnesses looking at them together. I'm not sure how much you want me to tell you at this point..

The disorientation you describe from the suddenly unobscured views at the forest is a bit like going into a neighbour's apartment, looking out their window at the same street or cutout of the sky you see every day from yours, and not understanding how a view so familiar can shift at all, let alone look completely different.

You write beautifully and I enjoy reading it all. I'm now picturing you in that big bed, surrounded by everything you described, and imagine your face illuminated by a screen as the view outside and the room around you slowly turn dark with nightfall.

Mon 10:59pm

I had just written you a long message, but when I hit send it failed to do so, and now it has disappeared. I'm very sad. It included what I learned from Sheila Heti's motherhood, a fantasy, and me telling you that I think you are gorgeous, but in better words. I will try to see if I can reproduce any of it tomorrow. My eyes are slowly closing.

Tue 12:09am

I felt unsatisfied, so here is my attempt of reproducing what I had written. It is late, hence any spelling mistakes.

-

In bed, again, after a day with students mostly spent by me and them staring out the window – but I doubt that they were fantasizing about some woman they met online.

You're gorgeous. The dutch light suits you. Velvet and satin in black, I don't think they can be mismatched, for they have sprung from the same delicate source. I am delighted to be Wittgenstein's Mistress to a corvid. I haven't read the book, but I will.

I have to think about loneliness. The experience of being the last person on earth somehow doesn't resonate with me, so I wonder if it could be an opposite: the feeling of not being a person at all or maybe a feeling of being the only person that ever existed (opposite of being the last person).

Sheila Heti's Motherhood has not taught me much about motherhood, but the more about the importance of making decisions, and of those decisions having (visible) consequences. And there is the problem in deciding whether to have or to not have children: the decision to have children is active – you decide on 'yes' and start trying to have a kid, and even when it fails, you had made a clear decision – whilst the decision to not have children is somewhat passive – it remains open for questioning (by yourself and society) until you cannot have children anymore or until you decide on sterilization, which can perhaps help to stop thinking about it, but is still invisible. The decision making has to happen in a time-window of say 20 years, even longer when you have frozen your eggs. I imagine women to have children just to not have to think about it anymore.

(this was my note to self)

My question on where your mind had drifted was not needed: my mind had already drifted from the blue light to the forest, and still lingers there, unsure which scenario to choose, delighted with the possibilities.

Disoriënting is indeed your view from a neighbour's apartment, as is waking up: the first seconds in which it is unclear what sort of day it is and its purpose. Then the specifics come in - tasks, hours, a schedule, people to meet - but only shortly after, feelings are attached to them, and you know what day it is, what you are supposed to do, how you feel about that and how you feel about your feelings. By then you have become a person though in those first seconds, you could have been anyone and maybe anything, a limitless body.
My small delusion: I believe I am capable of moving objects without touching them, if only I would practice and find the focus some day.

A pleasant disorientation is what befalls me when i'm on the near empty train, reading your thoughts as dawn rides along on the other side of the glass. it is easy to get lost in both. it is disorientation i feel most comfortable in - being still in. it makes me restless when nothing around me moves, when there is no promise of surprises or openings. here i fall into your words like i imagine slowly and ever so softly disappearing into your skin. revealing something new with every second and third glance, and so on - an image of something unknown crystalizing in response to being observed carefully. i imagine easily spending a long time tracing the bones on the back of your hand under your skin with the back of mine, nothing else. I want to see what unsatisfied looks like on your face when you lose a long message you wrote to me on your phone, and i want to see what delight looks like on your face when you get lost in thought between blue light and the forest.

don't worry too much about losing messages. even if you take a long time to write anything to me, i wouldn't assume anything bad. and for god's sake forgive me all my spelling mistakes too. so bad...

there is too much to write on the topics of Wittgenstein's Mistress and on motherhood - both your and Heti's views on it. I will say I vehemently disagree with the one-sided point of view that choosing to make a child is an active choice and that not having any is a passive one. don't forget that choosing to have them means not having the experience of any other kind of life, of which there are many and almost all undervalued and insufficiently explored.

i sincerely hope at least one of your students was also fantasizing about some person they'd met online.

You probably already can move objects with your thoughts, you're just not around when it happens.

What was the last painting you lost yourself in? I'm rediscovering this wonder atm and contemplating a trip to Madrid just to see it.

https://en.wikipedia.org/wiki/The_Garden_of_Earthly_Delights

Thu 09:27am

Forget my use of active-passive, I see it wasn't helpful here in expressing myself. What I tried to say is this: when a woman decides to not have a child, no matter how loud her no, for 20 years (or longer) she will be asked the same question over and over again, be told she will regret her choice for she must change her mind, as if yes is the only correct answer according to society. When a woman has a child, she would never be asked to re-evaluate her choice, be asked "do you regret your choice? will you keep your children? or will give them away, get rid of them?"

I was not trying to say something about the value of lives with or without children. It is the extended moment of decision that I'm currently interested in, and a 'no' that is not taken for an answer. But motherhood seems a complex and delicate topic, not so suitable to be discussed via this interface.

I collected things for you the last days: a red transparent lighter lit by moonlight, stepped over in a brussels bourgeois neighborhood while on my way to a birthday party in a pizza place - a large open space with big pieces of furniture awkwardly pushed aside to make space for tables, looking like it was by day a store for garden decorations, the personnel having forgotten about guests coming that night until someone asked for a pizza margherita - in that same space a poinsettio wrapped in cellophane, a long table occupied by my friend's friends: a group of joyfull women who had just had the final rehearsal for a performance piece, speaking in greek about magicians and improvisation. On my way back an almost 4 meter high front door in dark blue, the triangle shaped window in the door panel and the stained glass window above the door together creating the shape of a giant key hole. The surface of the house, grey stone, seemed painted like wallpaper giving the 4 story building the appearance of a madhouse to be found on a fun fair. I was sure it had a room somewhere with an antique bath on paw feet - I imagined you in there.

On monday, I followed a pair of black patent leather heels through the corridors of the subway station.

I will stand behind you when you get lost in the painting, my chin resting on your shoulder. There is a photo series of me somewhere, taken by an ex-lover a decade ago, recreating small scenes from the garden. Somewhere in the grass, there is a woman who's head is a birdhouse.

You can live in her head if you wish.

You look like a mirage that forms by night- beautiful and otherworldly in the dressing room light. The clothes of Wittgenstein's widow suit you, minus any sadness or loneliness.

I am very comfortable now, enjoying listening to my surroundings and receiving your pictures. I will write more later when I've composed my loose thoughts of the day into a coherent trail.

A while ago I was at a very small and intimate artist talk by Adrián Villar Rojas. It was an early morning that felt like the first hour of winter. If you haven't seen the installation he made here, don't look it up. it's what i want to show you the 28th, and all the more special if you don't know what to expect.

I look forward to adding your rescued lighter to my collection of personal talismans and found trinkets that inspire new works. and of course i was there in that building - most likely it disapeared after you left - sunken into a bath, listening under water to your steps stopping in the street below.

was it Sophie Calle you followed in the leatherette subway maze? did anyone follow you? how did it end?

and let's look at the painting together.

Fri 10:13am

on tue-thu I get on an early train and work out of town. the views from the train are pretty and i'm usually on it when the sun rises. my wish is to ride the train with the lights off so we can enjoy the dimly lit view instead of our own overlit reflections in the window. when i come home on thursday, I feel like an animal that was transported in a box, and need a day to stretch out my limbs and feel like myself again. between now and tuesday morning i am free and in my most natural mode; there is always work to be done in my studio, and my imagination steadily devours the future into reality.

yesterday i saw a man who in a flash looked exactly like Samuel Beckett, but cleary was just going about some very mundane business, and a pain shot through me as i felt how terribly fragile this balancing act is of creating one's art whilst surviving and what terrible loss it would have been if Beckett had resigned to an ordinary life like the man in the street.

going back to your poignant image of being at home under water in the bath, with air being the other world; i feel like they could also represent two states - one being the ecstasy of feeling at one with everything in the real/outside world, the other of being immersed in the depths of the self. the past three (or more) years have felt like all was suddenly turned inside out, and i have this year come back into the air, transformed. it is not the first such transformation i've been through, yet they have all been completely different; not like the snake shedding its skin over and over again, but as if i turn into an altogether different animal each time. this last transformation has given me the gift of seeing my own past in a new/different light. this painting - like dark baths - is what I call a talisman of homesickness or belonging. I grew up seeing it every day and it became part of my body, before i knew what it meant. I took it as a given, no different from trees, or cabinets or air. now it is a trigger of my deepest self beyond the narrative of memories and nostalgia - along with many other works of art and phenomena from the iron side of the curtain ;) I'm delighted that you have a connection with this painting. if you look at it with me, you will see one of the substances i was made of and i will see it as a painting for the first time.

indulge me one last thought on the topic of motherhood on this interface. I wasn't vehemently responding to you, but in my mind to all the unsolicited questions and opinions of others you described so well in your response.

And please look beyond my talking a bit too much about myself now, but I find it too overwhelming to talk about art here the way i want to, so i'll leave that for actual conversations.

Sat 06:40pm

Since I am interested in you, I find you talking about yourself to be very pleasurable.

I got lost in the logistics of life and found myself cleaning apartments, packing stuff and attending christmas dinners. Since a couple of hours I have landed again in the apartment where I'll more or less stay until my move to Rotterdam - where I can sit on the roof just outside my window drinking coffee, where autumn has revealed another historical building behind the garden, and where I trace the remains of a relationship, my friend that lives here having broken up with her partner just before she left, a nail in the wall where their picture used to be.

The woman in the metro seemed from a different realm than her feet wearing the shoes - millennial pink pants combined with a dark beige down jacket with fur collar - and I wondered about her secret other life.

It wasn't Sophie for sure. I wouldn't have known what to do with her, make her walk up and down til eternity, and left her on the platform.

I am somewhat struck by your talking about shedding skin, transformations and residing in disorientation. Shedding skin is how a friend described my practice and life: I am unable to hold on to objects for too long, for I want the outside world to reflect my transformations on the inside, and yet I will always remain unsatisfied, wanting to become something or someone else. I leave clothes and objects wherever I go, always carrying something with me that I want out of my life. I don't leave traces: the object had to disappear from sight entirely.

Perhaps you enter cocoons, since the transformations seem so radical. I'm curious about how you narrate your life.

Just some days before you mentioned Samuel Beckett in a message, I had googled an image of him, since I realized I had no idea of what he looked like. I am at a point in which I fear slipping into the role of language teacher forever, and yet I find it important to live in different realms at once, as long as I can also be the person translating these realms into art.

I hope you have smoothed out your wings by now and have landed too, somewhere in a state of mind that bemuses and delights you.

Sun 02:33pm

I'm watching Hunger by Steve McQueen, trying to hold on to a mood so I can write or change the direction of a work in my studio. For now the mood is fickle and eludes me. I might watch Shame as well.

One of the things I'm doing: I cut words - not letters - from magazines, mostly art magazines because those I already have a ton of, but I prefer to hunt for better words in more obscure publications, brochures, smut, cheap stuff. I lay the words out on big tables and start to arrange poems. If I make a good one, I photograph it and reuse the words in other poems. I also just write poems, and these cut-ups are very different from those. The cut-ups are things I would never think to write from scratch. It's more playful, but the end result still has to hold up. I'm quite strict and don't do short cuts, easy gratification or superfluous.
I'm curious how you separate your two worlds of being an artist, and being a teacher if you don't 'multitask', as you put it. Is your artistic practice entirely dormant for months? Do you keep notes in some form?

The transformations I mentioned are fundamental, but perhaps not as radical as they sound. It's what happens after great emotional events, when the subtleties of perception, action and the interior scale of things irreversibly shift or sharpen - but then again, subtleties are everything, and their ripple effects reach far. We'll have to talk about disorientation sometime. I think it is a subject of great interest to both of us.

I'm curious where your restlessness (?) comes from. Is it about finding what you desire, or about finding out what you desire?

I like your bangs.

Mon 12:04am

I grew up in an image of stability; but inside that suburban home was a lot of anxiety and restlessness. This last year, I have used the Villa Volta - a madhouse in amusement park De Efteling in the netherlands - as a comparison. It tells the story of a home that has been cursed in order to punish its inhabitant: it's interior is constantly turning around its axis, the floors become the ceiling that becomes the walls - making it impossible to orientate yourself. My parental home has always been like this. On the one hand literally - my mother was constantly moving the furniture around, painting the walls and doors, putting wallpaper, redoing, refurbishing, renovating. On the other hand, by affecting us with her fear of the outside world, by not trusting us to take care of ourselves, taking things from our hands, disencouraging attempts to take risks and explore. My father would remain quiet, but have sudden outbursts of anger.

My parents are also very calm and friendly people, but unfortunately, they have never been able to build confidence in each other and in their kids.

I wasn't done with my message and hit send by accident. This was not intended as a rant. I will continue writing now.

So, it is from there, a home that is appears to be stable but its insides are moving, that I entered the world, and that causes restlessness I suppose. But simultaneously, my restlessness is motivated by searching for growth, and wanting to be more than safe and secure but afraid. So I challenge myself.

Knowing what I desire, fear of that desire, multitasking, a dormant practice, making outside of institutions, too much embodyment concerning my work, art and career, art as therapy, are all questions that I am currently figuring out - or they will always remain a question, which is ok.
Today I took a bus to a bus stop with the most wonderful name - Calypso 2000 - after which I participated in a family constellation. In the first session, I represented one woman's ex-husband. In the second - my life is haunted by houses - we tried to help a woman figure out

whether she should sell or sublet her home in Argentina. I represented long-term sublet, and stood securely by her side.

The image of you taming, shuffling, hushing, guiding cut-out words into poems is soothing. It makes me think of you as a patient person sweeping finished poems of the table for the pleasure of entering a new game.

I won't google Adrián Villar Rojas. I promise. And I like that you like my bangs.

Calypso 2000 sounds like the title of a new work. there is an equivalent of this in the northern part of ams; a seedy and perpetually closed-looking
place called 'PARADISE' (big all caps, italic, red) on an industrial lot. Its only window facing the street is big and a one-way mirror.

the family constellation reminds me of 'Synecdoche, New York'. did it feel that way?
I'm considering changing your name in my phone to 'long-term sublet'.

This time I'm the one who's struck by your descriptions of your past and home. There is much that I recognize, but never thought to articulate the way you have. I look forward to spending time in each other's company, and following these trails of thoughts uninterrupted.

I hope you settled into your new place for the time being, and find humor or inspiration in the silhouettes of erasure that share it with you. If you are teaching today, the windows of the classroom are looking at you.

Tue 11:27pm

A short message that I hope will travel with you on your train ride in the morning. I'm in bed, too tired to formulate phrases, just some slivers

//A man - 70 years old, sportshat, sneakers, 80's jeans, windbreaker - at the tram stop, listening to his tarot predictions for 2020 on full volume. He was a Capricorn. The High Priestess awaited him.

//I have only two students left and I'm counting down the days til I can take the train that signals I have a holiday, that I don't have to explain grammar for two weeks, that I will meet you soon.

//I have been moved to a new classroom. On the windows: christmas stickers that my colleague has secretly put there. I don't think these windows are watching me, or I don't want to be watched by them, because of the stickers.

//So I try to connect with the ravens in the forest.

//And they fly low as I run in a loop.

//The experience of the constellation was indeed a bit like Synecdoche, but Meghan, our guide, prevented the house market from collapse.

//Although I consider myself to be reliable, I prefer to stay Wittgenstein's Mistress in your phone instead of long-term sublet.

//Goodmorning

Wed 10:11am

Good morning

The class room windows with creepy christmas stickers are NOT looking at you ;) Since you mentioned looking out and fantasizing about some woman you met online, I thought it'd be nice, but this is not the mood I was going for. The ravens of the forest on the other hand, I'm sure watch over you with curiosity.

I laughed out loud about mr Tarot. How wonderful. No doubt the High Priestess awaits him at home in full regalia, with all-seeing eyes, where they steer the fate of humanity from their small kitchen table with a colourful table
cloth, and a solo ashtray for her cigarettes. I am also ready to finish work, have time off, and meet you.

last night after work i left a poem breathing on the table in my studio. I couldn't sleep - occasional sleeplessness is a new thing that shadows me like a puppy I don't want to name - but the poem being in good shape soothed me and will continue to do so on this disjointed day. On my way out I grabbed a thin volume of Sylvia Plath poems - mainly for its size that fits my pocket. I'm not a Plath groupie, but she is good beyond personal taste, and a fine tuned palate cleanser if left unread for long enough - I opened it randomly while still on the subway and found a few perfectly strung lines:

What do wheels eat, these wheels

Fixed to their arcs like gods,

The silver leash of the will -

Inexorable. And their pride!

All the gods know is destinations.

I am a letter in this slot -

I fly to a name, two eyes.

I've arrived at my destination. the train stop is adjacent to a large open marsh with cows and sheep, and today even sunlight. The moon looms above it, white, big and weightless. I'm starting to wake up.

Your name remains unchanged in my phone.

Thu 10:06am

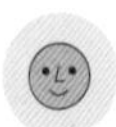

There is a word in Hungarian for the risk of getting a cold when you walk bare feet on a cold floor, but I forgot it, so whenever my feet sense cold tiles in kitchens and bathrooms, I am aware that a word is missing. Perhaps this danger was never present in dutch and english kitchens, but since I know of it, I only let my toes touch the floor, as if the floor is lava and the carpets my safe haven.

Small and lightweight volumes are the best. It makes it effortless for the reader to intertwine its contents with realities, whilst big volumes never get to leave the house. They are bound to the memory and notes of the reader for being taken outside.

I will read Sylvia Plath's poem again when I myself am being transported. It seems that - in between the lines - the reader should see something new everytime they look up from the page.

I am mentally preparing myself - from my bed still, coffee close by, outside my window a tree with pigeons, my least favorite animal,

as they try to fly through my head or crawl in my wheel whenever I am on a bike, so recently I figured I must be invisible to them - for a lesson with tests and a christmas drink at work.
*my hungarian friend told me about the word. It might be that it only had relevance in her kitchen.

i too have the christmas thing at work today and am writing this from the train.

the word you are looking for is ‘felfázni’ and it literally translates as ‘catching a cold upwards’. A friend of mine is a doctor and he reassured me this is no superstition. more precisely it relates to getting a bladder infection from cold feet. not sure whether this applies to men though.

my grandparents constantly complained and pleaded about this with us (my mom, aunt and me). they had stone floors and we didn’t believe in slippers. in my grandmother’s eyes we were perpetually malnourished and underdressed.

there is a lot to be said about pigeons.

From the way you describe (not) touching cold floors, I feel like I know what your feet are like, even though I’ve never seen them - also like a word that only exists in another language.

You are probably the opposite of invisible to pigeons, that’s why they want your attention. Because of their reluctance to get out of harm’s way (or your bike) - lazily risking their lives instead of just flying away - I hypothesize that they are on an evolutionary path to becoming flightless birds. I used to dislike them too; the phrase ‘rats of the sky’ along with their apathetic facial expression somehow justified my aversion. Then something changed - someone clearly less jaded talked sweetly and fondly of them, no differently than they would about any

other animal. I felt silly and started to see them in this benevolent light. They still annoy the shit out of me - i even wrote a poem about this - but I no longer see them as pests. I hope my going soft on pigeons isn't a deal breaker for you... hehe.
How is Brussels on a Thursday night? What are you wearing?

Synthetic snakeskin covers my legs, my upper body warmed by bits of a cashmere goat. Between me and the floor are suede, wool and cotton. Hair is braided. Look in general: casual loungewear for a yoga teacher with a lover that is in some soft rock n roll band. Or: gwyneth paltrow trying to relax.

About pigeons. I'd like to distinguish between urban pigeons and the ones intelligent enough to remain in nature, as they are different species to me. It's not entirely the pigeons' fault they seem suicidal or just lost - they have adapted perfectly to our society, waddling and hobbling away as mindless consumers in pursuit of fast food - the thrill of mayonnaise. Maybe that's where my dislike for them originates. That, and the many times I almost had an accident caused by their indecion.

To spend so much time disliking pigeons - trying to understand why we don't get along - can be an act of love.

What are you wearing? And how was your christmas thing?

Summary of mine: passionately talking about commuting to work - 'Terrible! The traffic!' 'So how many busses do you take?' + experiencing discomfort of others as I tell them, for the 20th time, no, I really don't drink. No, I don't want a glass of cava. No, I also don't eat meat. No, I really don't want any sausage, thank you. No, I don't find this difficult. Yes, I am perfectly fine. No, thank you, no sausage. No. Just. No, thank you.

Crowd for the vast majority consisting of (pensioned) flemish language teachers. The Flemish really like their beer and sausage.

*indecision

I'm no longer wearing shoes. thin black extra soft cotton socks around my feet resting on the couch. my synthetic almost black dark green pants already unbuttoned after the first christmas meal of the year and my first proper meal in a long time. soft black cotton between me and the pants. hidden layer of monochrome lace under two layers of cotton on top - one mauve, one white. wearing my hair down. it's wavy from rain earlier. russian red lipstick. I don't know what I look like. a fire?

My christmas thing was pleasant. I work at a small publisher of social study books for high schools. It's a mixed bunch that spans the spectrum from locals who've been doing office management for this publisher since day one (25 years), to teachers, academics, journalists, digital workers, a graphic designer, a drummer in a punk band, and a literary translator- almost all work part time and do other stuff as well, all aged between 28-70, some gay, most not, none foreign except for me. They are used to dietary preferences, so no hassle about not drinking and (not) eating meat. They did make us sing which is my nightmare.
The staff got a box of gifts -mostly kitchen related - which is weird because I'm very minimal and never keep stuff in the kitchen / bathroom that I don't use. I can't say that I cook. Bringing this stuff home makes it feel like someone else's kitchen.

'suicidal pigeons' and 'thrill of mayonnaise' are such good band names.

The thought of you receiving excess stuff for your kitchen makes me nervous. And it's not even my kitchen. I probably would bring it to the thrift shop or give it away the day after. My friends have stopped giving me gifts some years ago, there's just no point. Sometimes they try, but end up taking it back. I'm very bad at faking enthusiasm.

I just had to conclude that my chick peas have soaked two days too long - I couldn't bring myself to cooking them - and will now have to throw them away. I could have known.
I hope to one day publish a book titled 'Cooking Without Passion'. It will be an anthology of artists/writers who take a stance against the cult of cooking. Your contribution is welcome.

I'm not sure it it's fire you look like, but the thought of you lying on the couch, your pants unbuttoned and thinking you are a fire made me laugh. Maybe you look like rocks along the east coast in Scotland at night, your hair moving as the water moves, dark green seaweed in murky waters.

I think I know that lipstick, it lies on the table near the entrance.

I'm sorry you had to sing. We share a nightmare.

you are funny. my contribution to your anthology will be passionate and short and will possibly be titled 'thrill of mayonnaise'.

Sat 04:16pm

Yesterday on a brussels' street: a priest in soutane searching for answers and directions on his smartphone.

Your tangerine sky makes me long for the day we didn't have. Only half an hour until sunset, and I have only just gotten on the train that takes me home. All that black silk makes me long for observing your movements traced by the fabric.

A man entering the train, asking in which direction the train will take us. People point to both front and back. Satisfied with this answer, he says: "Good to know. I would like to go forward" and continues his search for a seat.

I would like to write more, but my mood today is particularly dark and gloomy and I am annoyed by everything and everyone. So, I will keep to myself for now, though in the virtual company of Audre Lorde, who made this journey a pleasant one nevertheless.

I understand, and wish you a short mood on the shortest day of the year, which might have been the culprit.

Sun 01:45pm

Another reconstruction of a message that got lost.

Brussels' buildings people speech clothing seem covered in a thin layer of grey dust. When a line forms at a supermarket register people wait patiently - in silence. One has given in to the resistance of a systemic net a long time ago, knowing all movement will be pointless. Speak softly, make small gestures is the device.

Here, in my home country, what we build are say wear is painted in bright colors, keeping us awake. All is taken care of, all is in order. Yet we keep writhing in this net, that to us is not captivity but protection from an outside evil. We demand the net to hold us tight. When a line forms at a supermarket register: tongue clicking finger tapping loud sighing voices. We demand to be assisted smoothless service denouncing resistance.

Stone dogs and cats survey the empty streets. A bright butterfly stuck flat to a brick wall. I wonder how you inhabit these wetlands. As the train moves south, the voice composing this message is bombarded by a choir of male voices, smell of beer large bodies swallowing us all. To not disappear in these hollow bodies, hoping the train will take me elsewhere. I speak soft voices make small gestures.

there is rarely any dust on anything outside here - courtesy of a regime of bicycles and too much wind and rain. finely dusted, grimy cities remind me of Budapest; perpetually grandiose, covered in a film of smog - the pesky and hazardous sign of 'things more important than your health are taking place' to remind people of their place in it.

I survive by examining edges and no-man's lands in between - the transitions where boundaries once reached turn out to be real or not - and find that the outside world has few to none, and that those of my inner self are soft, moveable up to a certain extent, and that any hard edges found there are priceless and important.

leave the loud beer bodies be, they too are fragile, though may not or never know why or how they or others are broken, as won't we of them. hardness is best met with ease, but this can be painful and not always without danger. I only speak for myself in this, but I've seen others do it and it is a compass for my own behaviour, although not always within my capacity. It is possible that you feel this way because you are in the wrong place. Location is important, and while these wetlands afford me relative freedom, and a home where I can close the door to the outside world, it does not and never has been a natural match to my inner world and sensitivities. Neither is the place I'm from at this point. I have thrown my anchor into myself and take it with me wherever I go. France feels good. I might move there, but not without means.

Today, as I distance myself from office work - with two weeks free of time-keeping stretched out before me like a magical and hazardless landscape - I find myself questioning the nature and existence of patterns. Everything we ever see and experience is new every time. Your words on the society or systems we live in and didn't create, but feel powerless to overthrow, are poetic and true. On the other hand we are free to do as we please and this is confusing as we are humans who find strength in the actions of others when they match our own desires, but are also often held back when they are not mirrored.

I hope your mood has lifted or, if persistent, a source of inspiration in some way.

I look forward to shooting the breeze with you in black silk and snakeskin, our heads infused with morning art and the back streets of the abandoned city - I don't have a bike and walk everywhere.

I've been reading Baudelaire and shuffling words in my studio. Now I will shower and go outside with a new playlist on my phone, and hunt for a vending machine hot chocolate, which I like better than most proper ones.

Mon 11:07pm

The taste of that particular hot chocolate on my tongue, sweet but sharp, slightly textured. I am sewing at my parent's place, for the sake of doing something. It is almost silent here - I don't know how their stereo works. My mother shows me the muesli that she has bought for me, and gives me an elaborate explanation of why she bought this particular kind. I tell her it's ok.

Today I picked up the remains of an artwork of mine that has been removed from a playground: two banana peels made out of ceramics, one intact (the spare banana), the other one marked by violence of play. It is a long story that I will tell you someday. The woman from the art committee gave me a bouquet of flowers: file closed.

The mood has lifted.

I thank you for your descriptions of your inner landscapes, I will walk them.

It is as if I don't know how to write to you, from here, my childhood home. I am in the attic, in a single bed. The attic - for Bachelard: a space that is inhabited with ratio, where dreams are met with hard edges - that holds my possessions stored in plastic crates, that keeps my parents' excess out of sight, that shelters material evidence of ancestors

- I was not done writing. To be continued...small technological challenges -

The attic in the corner of which I built a home for myself in this house: sheets, a few objects from a box that said 'decoration' and of which the contents were used in rotation. It was a small space under the roof behind the dryer where I covered my need for privacy. I would go there after school and sit there in my tent, arranging and rearranging the objects. That was all. Sitting and moving objects, searching for a moment when all would be in it's right place - that never came, but was the start of a process that still goes on.

And if my description of the attic appears as romantic, and if it creates an image of old books, wooden floors, antiques and treasures: it is not. Imagine this attic in bright colours, in plastic, in ikea furniture, in attempts of adding personal touch, in practicalities and most of all, in a large variety of storage solutions, neatly organized, categorized, sorted, archived, stacked and well kept and mostly within reach and labeled.
Crafts. Christmas decoration. Camping gear.

It is from here that I try to reach you. But I only exist partially here - my archived self, two white boxes with my name written on them.

Words are different, and limited. Here, I listen, to my becoming from under layers of familiar chatter. To the same stories. To the same coughs, burps, sneezes, sighs that accompany annoyance, relief, anxiety, sadness, sometimes happiness. To intimacy that comes from being together, and that is demanded by the house, by the thin walls, lack of doors, the large bodies inhabiting the space. My voice is different, it bounces off the diagonal walls and veers back fifteen years ago.

It is from here, that I try to imagine meeting you, but I am only sixteen, and haven't tried out my voice yet.

Tue 12:45am

I'm glad you've crossed the border. It feels adventurous that we are both on the same side of it.

I can see you, at 16 and now in that unromantic attic that you inadvertently managed to make romantic by infusing it with your layered presence and perception.

If you think writing to me from your familial attic is strange, imagine that we will soon switch to speaking Dutch, both in an entirely new incarnation of our voices.

The top floor or attic, according to Slavoj Zizek, is the representation of the superego in Bates' house on the hill - the ground floor the ego, the basement the id. Houses haven't been the same to me since. Thinking of the basements of 'Im Keller' by Ulrich Seidl, I can't help but believe they represent the collective and repressed subconscious of Austria.

Bachelard's 'Psychoanalysis of Fire' is on my nightstand. Walking the long way home from 'contemporary' sushi with a friend, I heard, smelled, but didn't see fireworks.

After dinner we went to her house. She cut my hair as her cats curled and watched our every move.

(the spare banana) is another good band name. I'm curious about the backstory to your artwork and its size...
Will you come read my interior?

I'm curious about the type of muesli.

We could agree on whispering or only using adjectives.

So, the muesli is actually cruesli. It is the one with nuts in a blue Quaker box. It is important that it's in a box, because apparently, when it's just a plastic bag, you lose ALL hand-eye coordination and motor skills - you basically turn into a 3 month old baby - and EVERYTHING will fall out of that bag! Everything! Imagine, the cruesli will be everywhere except in your bowl! Don't you ever buy muesli again that is not in a cardboard box. It will make your life hell,

Today the harsh morning light revealed to me that the powder I put on my face on a daily basis gives me a yellow hue. I hope you like yellow.

And, yes, I will come for an analysis of your interior. I consider it crucial.

I like your face. I'm pretty sure it's the same in yellow. My sun-starved complexion borders on translucent at this point. I hope you like glow-in-the-dark.

I like transparent and translucent things, though I have just sold kartells 'ghost chair' that I owned, that was supposed to be the start of my interior of transparent things, after Nabokov. My eyes have gotten a special sensitivity for glow-in-the-dark thanks to 90s bedroom deco for children, so I can perceive you well. The powder that I use is named 'healthy powder'. I too am sunstarved underneath.

Wed 02:11am

The ghost chair suits you.
Glowing in the dark does sound fun. There's a great creepy painting by Tyra Kleen called 'Nocturne' of two laughing glow-in-the-dark skeletons gliding across the surface of a moonlit lake, arm in arm in white dresses while one of them smokes and the other one fans herself.

Tonight was my first family christmas dinner. It was the chaotic one at my Hungarian aunt's house; lots of talking at the same time in three languages, mostly classical music industry gossip, health talk, gossip about people's difficult neighbours and domestic woes, whatsapp video calls to people abroad, what luggage sizes constitute carry-on, what movies to stream, piano playing, dog waiting for treats, cat waiting for attention, all while eating the foods of my childhood. Tomorrow another big dinner, but at my friend's family. A different kind of heartwarming mood - more highbrow french menu, less nostalgia.

Did the very large fold-out table fold out?

We have to get a BAG of muesli, cut it open ALL wrong and unleash mayhem. Preferably in your kitchen. I always get buckwheat flakes. It comes in a messy bag.

Muesli mayhem is...another great band name. Food seems to work. Throwing around muesli seems a desirable alternative for my christmas til now.

My father did not fold out the folding table this year, because my aunt and uncle won't visit: they bought a house last september (!) which means that you are so busy renovating that you cannot free yourself one evening for dinner. I don't mind really. I don't think

I have learned conversation skills from my parents. The last days I spent screaming inside while they 'discussed' feminism, religion and other fun topics. The word 'listening' doesn't exist in their vocabulary I'm afraid. Both my parents claim the other is attacking them before the conversation has even started. Overall a lot of sexism, racism, homophobia.

Watching television together is another fun activity. My father manages to insult everyone on tv by some misplaced joke.

I have just fled the house. We had breakfast together for christmas, and before 11 I had already heard at least two racist terms.

What is most frustrating, is that neither of them (my parents and brothers) of them seems to be able to articulate, give arguments, or admit that they are wrong on at least some points. These arguments become a vehicle for family issues, at the cost of others.

Now I am on my way to friends, my company of choice for christmas.

Sorry for releasing my anger into this chatbox. It has taken over my brain.

Talking about carry-on luggage sounds lovely.

Thank you for mentioning the painting, I really like it. Enjoy french cuisine.

May I suggest an extra lap when you're running to dispel any anger that doesn't find (welcome) release in conversations, chats, notes, humor, works of art?

christmas is just a random holiday on steroids that for me holds fond childhood memories, but is personally meaningless beyond that. It gets easier every year to distance myself from its undesirable aspects.

This year I said no to the other (Dutch, non chaotic) family christmas thing - a four hour drive away - and decided not to overthink it. the family members are nice, the time spent together is pleasant, but I simply didn't feel up to it, and I didn't force myself for the sake of love habit guilt expectation whatever. I guess, without explicitly advising you on anything, I hope you realize you can say no and not go through family christmas on other people's terms. It sounds like a difficult situation to be in for an extended period of time. I'm glad a more desirable get together awaits you today.

You're right. Sorry to have put my anger here.

Indeed, I can say no, though this is a slow learning process, and I seem only to remember I should have said no when I'm in the middle of it.

I am with friends now, we're building a snow landscape out of white sheets.

No need to be sorry. I don't mind you telling me, it just sounds tough.

The landscape of sheets sounds liberating. Recommended reading material for your next train journey (if you haven't read it already) - Nick Cave on the life of sheets. https://www.theredhandfiles.com/what-oh-what-is-ku-klux-furniture/

Thu 11:43am

I fear my intonation may have gotten lost in this medium in the last messages. Your rants are very welcome here, and I appreciate you sharing your stories with me. I hope you don't think I was dismissive.

In general I find conversing over chat slightly confusing. You never know in which moment the other will receive your message. Often, the timing is off. This time, my anger and the moment in which I had time to write to you unfortunately coincided, and before I knew I had sent the message into the universe. Running another lap is always a good idea.

You asked me about paintings I had recently lost myself in. I don't get lost in painting so easily. I'd say I can get lost in the work of the aforementioned René Daniëls, though it is not so much a matter of looking at the painting itself. It's what's outside the frame in which I lose myself after seeing his work. This painting made my world tumble. It's part of a series called 'Springblossoms'. They depict what can be seen as trees, the blossoms being names of his paintings and places he has been. Simultaneously, it can be seen as the map of a city or a harbour. Front view becomes top view. It was a small sentence on this painting that made me tremble: "wall for sculpture, floor for painting."

https://images.app.goo.gl/rgYw8i1rsoJCAJmi9

Another painter that I like for her offering of multiple perspectives is Jo Baer.

At the Boijmans museum, there are two paintings that I have to check on whenever I'm there. 'Mandril' by Oskar Kokoschka and 'De Schiettent' by Pyke Koch. I don't like leaving the museum before I have said hello to the monkey and the lady, but often I get lost at the Boijmans, which leaves me walking nervously through centuries of imagery before I can go home and experience fulfilment.
https://www.boijmans.nl/collectie/kunstwerken/3616/de-mandril

https://www.boijmans.nl/collectie/kunstwerken/2124/de-schiettent

In what sort of space are you? What occupies your mind at this moment?

I'm looking at Gena Rowlands strolling through a cemetery in a black silk Ungaro suit - black silk is becoming a theme - and at a string of lights outside moving with the wind. She has a gun in her purse. She has to shake off the maffia and save the boy's life. I will walk with you through your paintings after, or I might save them for my morning coffee.

In general my mind is preoccupied by a book (books) that are ready to print, figuring out how I'm going to do that. Part of my brain is always preoccupied with what I left in my studio / how I left it. I'm thinking about two close
friends in particular, but that's a story for another time. I think about us meeting.

Was last night good?

Fri 11:16am

between my first and second coffee:

these blossom paintings are simultaneously poems, and the lines that moved you are the pit of the whirlpool of this one. Thank you for showing me. I skidded over his oeuvre - my first impressions having been superficial, based on other paintings and a few sterile articles - but you shed a different light on them that opened it up for me.

Kokoschka's monkey reminds me of the joy of painting itself. colours being its joy, the specificity of its materials, the game of composition - i don't mean to imply there are rules, but when one paints, they are made. painting is something i haven't done in what seems like a lifetime. i am still examining how deliberate a choice this was on my part or if it is something that I actually deeply miss and am avoiding. I'm not convinced of the purity of the latter. there's too many

decisions that support the former scenario, but the second still crosses my mind sometimes, like a math problem to revisit or a touchstone for other dilemmas.
I'm a bit too minimalistic or abstract for Pyke Koch. The theme and colours of the background too dated for me to get lost in, but I imagine it with an ever so slightly lilac grey monochrome background covering everything but her, and the table with the rifles to bring out her torso, and the rich browns and the abstract arrangement of the rifles. A contemporary painting of a schiettent seems an exciting subject; the neons, fluorescents, modern clothing, grime, plastics and fluff. I find the hysterics of present day, traveling fun fairs enormously inspiring, and have a few (too) high-budget, monumental scale ideas shelved and waiting.

I will revisit Jo Baer with a clear mind.

Last night was good. I am lucky to have friends who insist on making a round of last years highs and lows during dinner, who welcomed some strangers, who then felt welcome and were happy to share their ideas and worries, friends that have had their share of trouble but bravely and stubbornly keep going, who were willing to participate in rituals burning the past and making futures out of clay - amidst a landscape built of whïte sheets (or what might be klu klux furniture).

Pyke koch is doesn't so much interest me on an intellectual or abstract level: it's mainly important that she is there, as a point of orientation.

I want to hear about your books, and what words are is living on your tabl
- what words are living on your table. And I look forward to uninterrupted speech.

See you tomorrow, a bit before ten, at quartier du putain.

See you then